Wilderness

Wilderness

Anna K. Ivey

RESOURCE *Publications* · Eugene, Oregon

WILDERNESS

Resource Publications
An Imprint of Wipf and Stock Publishers
199 W. 8th Ave., Suite 3
Eugene, OR 97401

www.wipfandstock.com

PAPERBACK ISBN: 978-1-5326-7883-7
HARDCOVER ISBN: 978-1-5326-7884-4
EBOOK ISBN: 978-1-5326-7885-1

Manufactured in the U.S.A.   APRIL 4, 2019

For Aralyn, my song. For Cade, my lion.

"In this my Scribble; nor did I intend
But to divert myself in doing this
From worser thoughts which make me do amiss."

"THE AUTHOR'S APOLOGY FOR HIS BOOK"
FROM *THE PILGRIM'S PROGRESS* BY JOHN BUNYAN

Contents

Acknowledgments

This project would never have come into fruition without the dedicated guidance of Dr. Beth Gylys. The inklings of this manuscript began with her generative workshop in the summer of 2016. The frantic pace of daily poetry production meant I would mine the rich ground of my own sins to keep crafting poems. Without her encouragement to keep delving into what mattered to me, I would have been too afraid to ever write about what I have here.

My beloved family—you are my dearest loves, my muses, my sonnets, my heart beat. My determination to grow was spurred on by your courage to do the same. I pray all of you know that at your cores, you are indeed loved and lovable.

Scott Wilkerson, thank you for soliciting a poem from me. "*El Hombre de La Mancha*" has a beautiful home with *Negative Capability.*

Tina Wilson, thank you for years of showing me God sees me differently than I do, and that rest matters just as much as work.

Borderlands

 Only it was no dream.

Those beestings came
every day—the terror of the next
argument, the shutting out
for weeks, the onslaught of depression
in her daughter, the threat of graduate school
failure,
post partum's vice grip.
Would she disintegrate, like bread in a pond?

She had been a two-legged
question mark in response,
in counseling, unhooking,
pulling knots out.

Before God could stitch wounds
tenuous, multiple, bone-unveiling, jagged,
she had to flee
her kingdom of the mind,
her safety in the thinking,
then maybe

her family could do
differently. She cooked meals, sweated for miles,
slept at the same time, swallowed

magnesium, vitamin D, B12, moringa olifera
to settle terror she lodged in
daily, hourly. She taught her girl
to love a hobby with so much fire
it ate the fear clean
as silver.

On the way to school, sky denim-blue and starlit,
she prayed over her children,
blessed them
to drop their burdens. She finally
got her nails done, visited friends,
allowed her husband
his anger,
stilled the motion in her being from the whisper,
It is not enough.

I.

"Shame tells me what men are; but it tells me nothing what God or the Word of God is."

THE PILGRIM'S PROGRESS

Barricades

Burying a father meant I next wrote all the truth but never slant. Imagined narratives collapsed: dead end plots flat characters tiresome dialogue. Deflated words, chewable like tires, were in tortuous details: *he got up and opened the door and walked across the room and took the glass of milk.* I ruptured with smidgens of imagery, patchworks of conversations, because that tension *was* mine—ugly, authentic. Poems came, current, exquisite, like *he is a semi-circle with pores of whiskey.* In verse I conjured exotic violence and the irony of politeness, since I swear any other narrative I hounded crumbled to smithereens.

Advocate

My girl goes drum-taut with worry
when her father leaves,
though she sees him only Sundays.
I call my brother Jonathan.
My God, it's just so hard
to not be angry. Her fear never stops.
I cannot keep this up.
He spiraled with venom after Dad died.
Mom, for years, sifted his fury
from his love,
intonating he must choose.
She has you and that will be enough,
he whispers, patient, knowing,
younger by six years.

He shares
his Meyers-Briggs type (INFJ) and love
language (quality time)
when locust-worry gnaws him about the woman
he loves across the country.
Yea, Campbell had me take those tests, he explains.
He's exactly like my girl.

He was always discerning,
Mom said.
He crumbled the knuckles
of an unwelcomed suitor after Dad died.
Gomer did not come back.

Aralyn has observed her Daddy
could do his job in the same state as her,
he moved away

exactly
when I remarried. I am shamed
by missing patterns for years.

I see it all and then I can't
fix it, my brother says.
I had to learn to let people hurt
if they chose it,
and let God have the rest.

No mother can be angry anymore at that.

Date day

So, the mother and her girl had to make
a second plan.

The cartoon movie about pets was sold out, so
the mother asked
her girl about seeing something else.
The daughter sighed like a fragile mermaid and agreed, but
the mother knew it wasn't what she wanted.

The mother tossed alternatives, confetti-like,
to her wide-eyed girl, who caught them between thumb and forefinger.

We can spend time talking if we aren't in a movie,
the mother explained.

Instead of stillness that afternoon,
the daughter climbed at the park. Sweat-scented
after, she drank the rest of the water the mother
had saved in the car.

The girl persisted she loved spearmint
and swore she'd water it, so the mother bought four herbs
half off and they planted them in the evening.

They visited the pet store
and the daughter glanced sideways at the parakeets
and her mother, then touched
the glass like gentle silk:
Oh, birds are so pretty.
Her mother shook her head.

After they split a scone and chai latte,
the mother said they could look at books for just a little while
longer.

The mother wept to her own mother,
It isn't fair she only has me.
Her mother admonished, *He chose*
this man to be her father. You must trust
He has purpose beyond today.

The girl slept that night and forgot her father
moved away and the mother
slackened her terror that she'd never love
her girl enough.

She didn't have to.

Ambassador

Aralyn usually has their number, the people
we meet. I make a game of asking in waiting rooms
what she makes of them.

That Daddy and his son aren't close,
she mentions in a Catholic whisper as we
wait to get her cast off her wrist.

*Yea, I noticed when he talked, the room
filled,* I add. She says, *The Dad is nervous
about being here. By himself without the Mom.*

The walls in that room are darling and clean
and she watches them come and go. I
check again if the therapist wrote back to,

*What do you do when you are so alone it burns?
How do you love anymore
when you are angry and dry?* I had to tell my girl

after voices compounded in the doorway
that we still cared but just didn't know
what to shoulder for the other. *We are trying, baby.*

I've told her that in dreams I sometimes
ask her to come with me on missions
to interpret the broken beings I see.

My prayers are strangled, pitiful.
God, all these shards of us now.

House cat

The cat was six weeks old when he came home
with a family. It was a present for the daughter. She confessed
later: *I really wanted the orange one. I wish I'd told you.*

They named him Neville Longbottom because the mom and stepdad thought
it would remind the daughter to be brave when her throat
clotted with fear of other people's anger.

Neville slept with the daughter for a few weeks until
the parents said he interrupted her rest. They made him
a nest of blue blankets he whorled into on the sofa.

He inhabited around the mother's legs and followed shadow-close to her
since she was home often. She would mumble with stolid lips
when Neville sowed litter across the floor. She had to block

 his food with chairs so the baby would not play with it. *Like I need one more
thing to take care of,* she muttered every other day. The daughter
handled the cat when she was home but most often the mother

did. The family found blankets soaked and reeking one morning,
Neville sucking the fabric. Disgusted and unaware,
the mother would toss Neville off her each time

he nestled on her lap at night, cloth-licking. After months,
she learned that cats do these things when they
leave their mothers too soon, so she started washing blankets without

another word.

Fit the bill

I.

An expensive career test insisted she would be
suited for engineering or law since
she preferred the order of things. *No interest in math, huh?*
said the counselor. He suggested to work
with adults if she changed
jobs—*You are so earnest*—and teenagers do little
consistently except lie
but she wanted summers and holidays with her daughter
and then could not imagine
anything except leading a classroom
with questions such as
How can God re-order
our concept of disability, as seen in The Miracle Worker?
How can the church use secular
tools to produce positive aims?
How can the epic Beowulf reveal
what Anglo-Saxons relied on for safety
before converting to Christianity?

II.

Volunteering at a pregnancy resource center, she learned
there were no stats on crisis pregnancies
and fathers who died.
Divorce, imprisonment, abuse
tipped
ragged-hearted women to terror with babies
they had not planned.

III.
Her beloved brother was the middle
child who hated
books. At eight,
he tried to give her money. When she didn't
understand, he cried because he had torn up her favorite
Indian shirt pretending to be a TV wrestler.
She wouldn't take a penny, laughed
gently when his guilt fell off like bricks. Years
later, he missed her wedding.
He wept regret after he got clean,
and she said, *But now you are here*
for all the days to come.

IV.
When she left her lover, her mother assured,
One day you'll meet a man
who wants you
and your girl. He will tear the earth down to have you.
God made someone strong enough
to do that on your behalf.
You must only wait.

V.
After six years of solitude, a man
did tear the earth apart for her.
She, poet born, went throatless
for words when he was ready
for the feelings she tucked aside like darling artifacts.

Learning curve

Words betrayed her sometimes,
when she doesn't use them and knows
she should. Those phrases,
lightning-slippery and invisible,
when it comes to him. Never
with her brother, her mother, her girl he notes. The folded
socks, the vacuumed rugs, the painted balustrades,
sincere as oaks, were not enough
because he hoarded gentle words in a granary
thick with unmet expectations.

*I see you sync with people, so I know
you can,* her husband insists.
He begs for her hands to come off her heart.
She only grips tighter.

Jonathan came back from Idaho
for a week.
At the knock,
she squeaked and clamored
while her husband drummed
fingers on his steeled thigh.

*I could disappear tomorrow and your life
would go on,* he monologued (again),
angry she vacuumed
early in the morning.
She couldn't chew out
it meant more she chose him
even as she retreated into
her own head.

He's asked me for my heart before, she said to the therapist,
but I can't give it to him.

Just give him time to learn, Tina replied.
Soon, you must risk as well. Love
cannot inhabit an airless box.

Acts of service and words of affirmation

Sometimes words are
venison jerky difficult and grow
thicker with use. The kids I teach get lost
in sentences
between their heads and the page.
I love nothing more than untangling together
so they know they have a story.

God gave us these tools, I tell them of words.
Tools form a home or tear it apart.
Words do the same.
The brain can make scrambled
eggs of punctuation commas spelling.
For a decade I've worn decoding
glasses and we reshape essays poems speeches stories to structure.
All of you have something
to say that matters.

I pluck and caress and chisel language
at home but my husband
finds sentences nuance-exhausting. *Sometimes*
I just don't know how to be nice, he says and I laugh
since words require nothing
of me. In a nuclear fallout
over if the baby should eat lumpy mush or not, words
are darts and arrows. I scream
for the first time all the phrases I hide behind my teeth.
I'd held old wounds, fistfuls
of wilted roses,
thrust them back to him
as he palmed dusty petals, astounded.

Scripture says you have to confront someone
if they have hurt you,
Tina says.
That is how you care for your own
heart.

We mourn in the silence after,
handing each other bricks through
gestures with no double meanings.

Not on board

She grinds her teeth against:
I may as well go alone.

Reasons mound: he wants to wait an extra week
before talking again, then speaks a pocketful
of words. He forgets. She schedules.
He complains,
It's all too time consuming as she aches on the couch
while he plays another rerun of *Mythbusters.* She
reads her book, sinking further under the stones.

But he's here, says the counselor. *He's here.*

Sons

He'd fortify his jaw, white knuckle them away, despise
himself when he spoke like memory.
The beloved called

long silences, divorce talk, *leaving right now,*
all punishment. *I won't accept it,*
she insisted, heartbroken he'd learned firsthand.

On a humid June, an opening chapter
about forgiveness needled tears from him. He excavated
his own apologies—though neither parent admitted

he should have been angry. But the words plucked
a few stones from his ribs. *No one gets an instruction
manual, honey. People do awful things when they are broken.*

Then she confessed she wanted a child
with him and he needed two weeks to measure through
terror and delight. His son came with pearl-blonde hair,

eyes just like his beloved's. He cleaned blood
and wounds for his wife and boy in days to come.
The beloved placed a hand on his when

she asked if he still felt anger, dull and metallic, now
that he had a little boy.
Well, they did the best they could, he said.

Snow in Henry County, Georgia

It's a running joke,
the South's hysteria in the cold.
When I go grocery shopping days early, bread
aisles are cleared, potato chips gone.

We diligent monks watch the forecast,
bewitched air staying a breath above freezing.
My girl tells me the next morning she was awake
on school time and went back to bed, disgusted at only ice.

The deck is shell-thick with glass,
flour colors mud. They warn against
travel, so today we fester with cleaning sorting rethinking.
At 2pm, Chad wears a sweatshirt to turn compost and fidget

with seedlings and churn minerals for spring soil. I
suggest he use boots I bought him four Christmases past. Two days ago,
he began speaking in therapy. Words uncurled from him like ferns.
The therapist told him I was too tired to discipline my girl

military-regular. *She's at capacity. You must save her
so she can,* advised the counselor and he sees me, petal-fragile,
 behind the calendar filled with appointments,
a file folder printed months before exams.

He laces up the first-time worn boots, once set near the peat moss bag
for growing the next season of plants—
the only conversation we never pretend
we care about.

Crux

They detonated once more with
dragon-fire anger.
This is it for me. This is all in to be here,
she said at an emergency
session with the counselor.
His anger uncurled
insane and cave-dark,
whorling
back to earliest days,
careening
into that very week.

She felt thickness seeping
through her legs, composing
her limbs to syrup
as when her father died.

She saw
the origin, the birthing
ground of where their destruction began—
the color of the first time he stopped
hugging her often, why
he didn't ask
how her daughter was doing.

I cannot be a wife to a man
with a heart of stone.
I will not
share you with unforgiveness.
I cannot carry this anymore.

I want out.

Dazed, astounded, he asked for three
ways to love her the next morning, so she said,
Forgive
your parents. God. Yourself.

He started with her.
She begged God for her wounds to shift
away from ugliness.
You were William Wallace
to me, she told him in the first tears
for months.
 But it must start somewhere.
And I am sorry too—

2.

"... without knowledge the heart is empty. But there are two kinds of knowledge: the first is alone in its bare speculation of things, and the second is accompanied by the grace of faith and love, which cause a man to do the will of God from the heart."

THE PILGRIM'S PROGRESS

General Anxiety Disorder

He told the therapist it could be "emotional instability,"
and I thought that was another
way to blame it all on me.
I asked if those weekly status
tests showed anything.
After all, my five siblings grapple
with thunderstorms in their own heads, too.

Anxiety affects marriage Chad, Tina says
the day we three can name it. *Help her
learn to manage it. Not for her. With her.*

As a child, I would stay awake—hours—
fixing fixing fixing my Christmas list
to not cost my parents much.
Once, a movie I saw suggested a mother could
die at any time. Anorexic, sleepless, I refused
to part with Mom, clogged with terror
soothing could not loosen.
In undergrad, I spiraled out for days
over a PhD dissertation a decade away.

Those bee stings of the mind, they come
when the to-do list hints
at avalanches: making dinner,
eating healthy, meetings back-to-back, papers to grade,
washing and drying my hair.

It's like I live inside smoke, I explain. *I can't hear
through it. But it quiets
when I workout and when I write.*

A friend says, *Your poetry I read*
is where you put your heart.
There is
another side.

I began to love my husband when he could
make me laugh.
Silliness eases threats
of unraveling over unvacuumed floors.
Two dates in, I saw a magnet on his fridge
that said his name meant *protector.*
Fog thinned enough
for me to wonder
if he could recognize
there is a woman buried beneath
a hurricane she generated with her mind.

More savage than the winds the rain
was my fear
he would find me.
I could not live within
barricades anymore if he did.

Fog

A wife began an education when she found
the fog, the knuckle cracking, the restless legs,
the cleaning on Saturday at 7am, the drowning in folding towels,
the *yes* to the unnecessary, the failure to remember, the agony
in change, the peeling nails,
the list keeping, the insistence *it must be done now*
for fear of overlooking a promise in an hour—
was blocking the view.

A husband's heart of rock became
silk as she admitted,
I can't remember not fighting this.
He was feather-gentle as he shifted
to how he must change.
We need a balance of me helping you
and me helping me, he says.

Instead of iron-hot resentment, on Friday
when she worked late to not grade
essays on the weekend, he picked up
their son without a second thought so she
could sweat, run, lift, through
remains of the hurricane
and see
into the weekend with her family the fog
did not veil.

Refurbishing

If a woman wants to change,
she can always start with the dining room.

The space was dignified, disused. She picked
the paint the curtain the cloth napkins

years ago to interlock, filling the home for only two.
I usually don't like this shade but I guess it isn't so bad if I don't

wear it, she told her mother of the rug she bought on sale.
They later used artwork from his home to finish the walls.

After a year therapy, she decided it was time
to use a new lens. The counselor told her things like:

You have to model what you want. Give love away.
People moved by acts of service don't want to ask—

it's like picking out your own
present and wrapping it. One Sunday

as her husband built a door for the garden fence,
she started shifting things around inside.

She read the week before no place in your home
should be unused, to reclaim

the rooms the attics the basements
that women often didn't know what to do with.

She added flowers, stored the placemats, left
out a single chair so she could write in the early

morning hours and still hear the baby.
On the wall she hung a wedding photo.

He peered in later, arms folded Egyptian firm, and said, *Yes,*
we need a space we do something with.

Art in the house

As I write nearby my family, words
ripen one after another. Oh my clasp before
on these verses,
the refuge in a two-hand tight
grip over softness my family could not have.
My husband watches my mouth
spool unspool as I hunt for
prepositions. He sips coffee. My girl
asks him questions he cannot
answer without researching.
The lines the stanzas still arrive
with everyone around and there is nothing so sacred
I must cherish it away from them altogether.
Both sleep better
as I become velvet.

Anniversary gift

He and I re-think grocery shopping
so we can be together on Saturdays.
Pollen powders the yard with blonde

dust when we have an entire day
with no one leaving. Nubby young hydrangeas
form a border under the left

windows. Seedless grapes, an almond
tree, golden raspberries came
in a box I could not hide.

I gave them to him weeks early.
*I thought it would be too late for planting
if I waited,* I said as he pulled

apart cardboard seams.
He asks again how tall
the almond tree will get. I have an answer

since I knew he would ask.
His words are sifted now with
gentleness. The fog peels back.

Essential oils, I learn, soak
cell deep, loosening a brain snapping
against a cavalry of threats.

The diffuser my Mom lends
protects my dignity. *It helps to invest
in a good one. But I've never used this,*

so try it and tell me if you like it,
what she does when she has no
plan to make good on a return.

He smiles when his gift for me comes before
it is time. I can only kiss him with delight
at a book he gives that says he loves me.

Clearing small trees
in winter in the backyard

With cracker-dry lips and our chainsaws hoist
above sweetgum trunks, we drink the shrieking
of devil thorns and gothic brush that voice
water burning from supple stems. Sinking
into the ashes mounding like cotton,
what is left of twenty years of neglect
we hack and push into flames. The lot on
the left is quite suave, emerald-perfect.
My husband, cut up like Christ from briars,
pushes gloved hands through his ash-speckled hair,
wonders whether to increase the fire's
height before rain makes it disappear.
We fell and formulate this square of land
each Sunday, side by side, with blade in hand.

Changed behavior

A man is a reimagined
human when a wife knows what
he needs. A man like this is cotton-gentle
if he rarely has to ask: leaving meals
when she's gone, turning on the heat lamp
for seedlings before he wakes, saving jars
for bursting avocado pits *(one day*
we can make our own guac!), pointing out flaws
in his plans *(honey, we should cut down more trees before*
you build a greenhouse), finding people
to get firewood that piles
like petulant aunts, boiling water for his coffee
thermos. Softness returns around the edges
of his eyes and he grabs frantically to pull
the words back if
they become razor edged. *I have tried*
my whole life not to be my parents
but I know it happens. Before, she sunk underneath
the job, the two children, the home,
the cleaning, the laundry, the groceries, the gym, the grad degree
and he'd be so angry when she insisted it was only hers.
She'd pull inward, let it spin around her
thick as galaxies. *It's like you go somewhere else,* he'd snarl.
On a Monday, she foresaw
the weekend overcrowded. Instead she reached
for him, *Can you help me*
about the recycling? That afternoon he loaded it into his car.
They went to sleep holding hands.

In common

Blending people is no small
feat. We began stitching how
to complete tasks—vegetables planting, berries pruning,
not wasting herbs. We craft garden walls, eight

feet, ground underlain with chicken wire.
I told him as he fretted over ground cover: *Get the rocks you want, honey.*
You should love the space we create. We scheme what to plant
in spring. For his birthday, I buy him a green canvas bag

It's for your garden tools and he later has me tickets
to *Phantom of the Opera* (*but it was from the kids!*) though
we swore no Christmas between us. At dinner with his family,
he tells them all casually, *Hey my wife has published a book!*

Braids

Burdens three years thick are lovely suitcases
to discard when a husband finally forgives a wife
for being a teacher.

Oh those thousand foxtrots waltzes tangoes
she numbed inside before.
I will never understand so much school for so little pay,

he says about teachers with doctorates. Executive minded,
he insisted since they married she must have
a next step. She can never argue with numbers.

A second job offer was her penance for the rocks
he carried with a career more fruitful than education
could ever be.

*I can't do more. I live inside fog and shards
of glass,* she wept in the driveway and he wasn't
angry this time.

Once, a husband
would have pulled the threads himself, ferocious with
disappointment.

But now he says vacation can happen
as they are. *We can't change
where we've been or the money we spent. All of this started*

before we met. I can live with that. The closeness to home, the meaning
in the job, the affordable tuition for the children
tip the scales that night.

She turns down the second job
as her husband takes the strings fraying, releasing,
then braids them back.

El Hombre de La Mancha

I.

We should bring back art, I had told him on our honeymoon
as we walked La Rambla in Barcelona. He found
Rorschach figures of Don Quixote and Sancho Panza
pressed against yellow.
The portrait was small, tourist-easy
to bring home. The air
was warm as cinnamon and the sea
nudged a blue shoulder towards the shoreline.

II.

As a girl, I remember watching
previews for *Braveheart*
and my father's breath slowed like a thoughtful bishop.
I can't wait to see that.
Back then, we did not
celebrate Halloween or watch *The Smurfs*
but he made the case, *She must see it.*
He closed my eyes at sex,
against decapitations, the shredded bodies.
Dad cleared his throat over and over at the ending
when William refused to bend.
That is what passion is, he said.
Years later, when it started to matter, I wanted
a man who would tear a world apart if
he were set on fire with love, like Wallace.

III.

I knew Chad would start fires just weeks after
we met. He, my lover, was a bringer of revolutionaries.
When I married him,
we kissed so fervently that people cleared their throats.

IV.

Do you think the yellow is weird? he second guessed
as I counted euros for the vendor. *I mean,
will it actually look alright anywhere in the house?*
I insisted it would. He grinned,
since we must use boldness to set the piece
on any wall we own.
Later, I stepped into the gelato shop
to order on his behalf in Spanish.
He held the picture,
eyebrow raised at all the words I summoned.
I knew what it felt then to be a thousand
mysteries to someone
who was unafraid of yellow—
or an uprising.

Self-medicating

My girl has been going with me for years
and would curl into corners like a patient
bird. Fingers laced into pages of *Harry Potter*,
she'd sigh and ask,
How much longer? about 30 minutes in.
You wanna be my counter? I'd try and she'd shrug
without commitment.

Hands floured with chalk, three times
each week I release
into sweat and movement. In this realm
where I have stillness
from the mental screeching,
words become guttural breaths
and salt. Eventually, she played nearby
on pull up bars and inspected rowing machines.
Eyebrow raised, she asked at times, *So, what are you doing?*
I have answers: *burpees sit ups*
snatches kettlebell swings powercleans squats
sprints shoulder press double unders goodmornings.
She'll count my reps, only when she forgot a book.

She got the flu for a week and festered with too much
time to think about how her father wouldn't change.
Baby, you must refocus on the good you do have,
I told her. *Notice how your body feels*
when those thoughts drown you.
God chose your Daddy for you
and there is purpose in it.

After her father missed her birthday,
she gathers her hair into her own hands, wraps
it into a ponytail and asks if she can
do what I'm doing.
We push back together against the voices
threatening undertow.

Harvest

A slow chisel flecked,
eased, pried the strangle hold
of worry off her daughter like barnacles.
Her mother prayed for years her girl would
not shoulder bricks
that were not her own. The girl spent weeks away
at Winshape camp each summer, easy in a different skin
with people who saw
even little girls have wounds
only God can mend.

In between summers, she didn't know
how to forgive her parents
and began to ask
questions that grated her mother's heart.
Was I mistake?

Her mother reached for her hand,
a question canyon deep for a car ride home.
My love, God tells us
children are a blessing,
no matter how we get them.
I was afraid when I first knew. I only saw
myself.
When people are scared, they
are ugly in what they think.
But your heartbeat on that screen,
you, a little grain of rice,
became my girl.
Then I wanted to move heaven and earth
to be your Mom.
God knew I needed you
before I did.

Aralyn's tears, thick as glue, dotted her jeans.
I've been so scared to ask you.
Her mother smiled and tucked her fingers
between her girl's.

In June, she went away
at camp for two weeks
again
and her mother wrote updates about home
where nothing special happened except ripening
peaches and talk of chickens.
Her mother picked up her girl on a Sunday.
Aralyn clenched her mother's neck and whispered,
Mama, I know. I know.
I know what it means to be a daughter
of a King. Fear
had dissipated into the humid air of pines.

If terror clawed to return,
the mother held her child's hand, reminding,
You know His love now
in your soul.
That means there is no need to be afraid.

Creative

She was reading Galatians—
those lines between the rules and the freedom.
After the children slept, her husband,
strange and timid, said he must tell her
something.

We have to know we are lovable,
we just have to trust that, he insisted.
Maybe that's the root,
he theorized. *If only Aralyn could remember this,*
if only we all could get this.
She smiled and the counselor later
said, *He understands now he is her.*

We fractured children,
cursed to wounds, to disease, to shame—
until He insisted it was worth it,
trading beauty for ashes,
renaming us to His family, longing for
us all to live
outside the shells of our armor.

Shalom

Months went by gently.

She was invited to read
her book and he insisted the children
must come. It was the first
reading he heard her do.
Writing is so lonely, she told them later.
I am glad you all were here. When
tears choked her with old words
about her father's death,
he bathed her in tenderness
in front of their son,
Let's tell Mommy we are so proud of her!

They talked about realms the other knew
nothing of: fantasy sports, teaching students
with learning differences, what sort
of vegetables grow through cold, whether
he should wear a watch, if
they should move away so he could be a farmer,
how to pay off the house
in 7 years, the shirt from Amazon she ordered
but didn't fit so she returned it, the cake he would bake for
Aralyn's birthday, all the cooking pans
she got since she threw a party to sell the products,
that she stalled out
on writing projects, he felt now
his parents did some things right,
if her Mom might like him to install lights on her deck.

I just wanted to tell you that you look happy now,
a coworker said.

At a school trip to a Bible museum,
in the giftshop she found a terracotta tile from Israel.
Glazed in white with petals
blue, yellow, green, and red, "Peace"
centered the square
in Hebrew black calligraphy.

She hung it in their kitchen, telling her family
There is no curse here anymore.

www.ingramcontent.com/pod-product-compliance
Lightning Source LLC
Chambersburg PA
CBHW072036060426

42449CB00010BA/2295